IMAGES OF ENGLAND

BIRMINGHAM
SHOPS AND SHOPPING

IMAGES OF ENGLAND

BIRMINGHAM
SHOPS AND SHOPPING

PETER DRAKE AND ANDREW MAXAM

TEMPUS

Frontispiece: A magnificent early view of the original Lewis's on the corner of Bull Street and Corporation Street. Looking back along Bull Street the next shops are Berrill & Sons, grocers, then the Minories and, just in view, Stead & Simpsons, bootmakers.

First published 2007

Tempus Publishing
Cirencester Road, Chalford,
Stroud, Gloucestershire, GL6 8PE
www.tempus-publishing.com

Tempus Publishing is an imprint of NPI Media Group

British Library Cataloguing in Publication Data.
A catalogue record for this book is available from the British Library.

ISBN 978 0 7524 4493 2
Typesetting and origination by NPI Media Group
Printed in Great Britain

Contents

Acknowledgements

The authors would like to thank local photographer Anthony Spettigue who has conducted a photographic survey of many of the remaining traditional shops and whose photos are now deposited with Birmingham Central Library. Nearly all the photos in the book have come from the collections in the Warwickshire Photographic Survey; a wonderful source of images of the city built up and looked after by the staff of the Local Studies section of the Central Library.

Another local history enthusiast, Kieron McMahon, has been helpful in providing copies of some of the images used in the book. Perhaps the greatest debt the authors have is to the anonymous agents for *Kelly Directories* who compiled the information for the annual directories which have allowed us to date and identify individual shops on what might seem a bland block of shops.

Below: A group of shops on the Bristol Road, Bournbrook, on 30 October 1950, including Keys shop, offering a strange mixture of cycles and televisions. Other shops shown here are a butchers, china and glass dealers, an ironmongers and a tailors.

Introduction

While we were compiling this book the *Birmingham Evening Mail* launched a campaign to save Birmingham shops. As the headlines on the front page of the paper on 15 August 2007 put it 'Warning as Small Shops Quit Birmingham'. The ensuing article blamed the internet, rising rates and cut throat competition for the dozens of empty shopping units in such formerly prime retail sites as Corporation and New Streets and the Great Western Arcade. This book is topical as we record both many of the famous Birmingham names which have already disappeared and some which are defying trends to hang on.

The Central Library commissioned a photographer to produce a record of Birmingham's independent shops to accompany this book and even while he was engaged in the project, long-established city centre and suburban shops were losing the battle to stay in business. Just this summer the long-established Bullivant's Drapery shop on Nechells Park Road finally closed to be replaced by a dentist's surgery and the piano shop; Alfred Allen's on Bristol Street was another to shut its doors. Of course we also include some of the winners in the constant battle to win the hearts and more importantly the purses of Birmingham shoppers and increasingly shoppers attracted to the city from further afield.

In a city the size of Birmingham, shopping is an activity which until fairly recently could basically be divided into two. One is going 'into town'. This would usually be a special day out, undertaken by public transport usually on the bus and would mean going to at least one of the main department stores whose location and reputation would be shared by everyone in Birmingham. At various times during the last fifty years the names would be Rackhams, Lewis's, Greys, Henrys, Barrows and they would all have their niche in Birmingham minds for a day's shopping in town. Now the same journey is as likely to be undertaken by car and it is likely to have one principal destination, the new iconic Bull Ring. The architecture of Birmingham's most famous building, with the silver clad spheres on the futuristic Selfridges building, is no less controversial than the arguments surrounding the effects of the concentration of so many retail shops and cafés within the one development. On the positive side, the number of visitors from all over the world are staggering, the volume of trade enormous and the facilities wonderful, but the Bull Ring effect has without doubt left its mark on the viability and character of the rest of the city centre shops and shopping arcades.

Shopping, perhaps more than any other single aspect of modern life, has driven the continual process of city centre redevelopment and hence has had the major impact on how Birmingham looks today. From the past in terms of the building of the inner ring road concentrating shopping in the city centre to the design and construction of the new Bull Ring to the future plans to redevelop New Street station and the Pallasades, the power of the retail lobby has been immense. As one of the directors of the oldest family-owned business in the city centre put it 'Birmingham has improved dramatically in terms of atmosphere and cleanliness but at the expense of being saturated by the five companies that own most of the city centre'.

The other main shopping activity would be at local shops in the district or suburb where you lived. This could be the archetypal small corner shop or it could be the high street with a mingling of independent shops and multiples of which some would be just Birmingham-based multiples. Or it could be the radial routes out of the city such as Newtown Row or significant inner city roads like Summer Lane or the Alum Rock Road, 'The Flat' in Hockley or the Ladypool Road. These days many of these local shops have gone and many of these roads have changed character in one wholesale redevelopment or another. The suburban high streets have changed character as well, as indeed they have all over the country. This process of the homogenisation of the high streets – Harborne, Kings Heath, Erdington, Selly Oak – leading to the loss of the small independent shop and its replacement by the estate agents, the kebab shop and the charity and pound shops seems to be remorseless.

It is not as if these developments were not foreseen at the time. Back in 1974 councillors on the city's Planning Committee commented on the loss of local shops caused by customers wanting to do a weekly shop by car. As the chair of the committee said, 'long strip shopping is dying in the city which means the loss of daily shops like butchers and greengrocers and the general shop round the corner'. Suburban shopping centres were thought to be the answer, some succeeded and others failed in the wake of competition from out-of-town rivals like the Merry Hill centre.

In more recent times a new vitality has returned to some traditional shopping streets in the city with the Asian takeover of many of the remaining corner type stores and the growing wealth of the city's diverse communities. Hopefully the images in this book will bring back memories of an era when shopping was a much more community experience and Brummies could either take a short stroll from their homes to the sights and aromas of their local shops or take the bus into town to enjoy the city centre's finest department stores.

Above: Joseph Riley and Sons.

Right: Station Street shops from Market Hall. A group of shops including Warmington, practical shirt makers, and James Watt and Co., successors to Satchwells furniture wholesale department. This view dates from 1946.

one

Department
Stores

Above and below: Contrasting views of one of Birmingham's main shopping thoroughfares in Corporation Street. The upper view shows the old North Western Arcade before the rebuilding of Rackhams and after the rebuilding, in 1932, of Lewis's on the corner of Bull Street. The second view from around 1972, shows the rebuilt Rackhams and North Western Arcade, left; a sale on at Lewis's; Maples furniture store to the right of Central Hall; and the roof line of the Martineau Square shopping precinct.

An early twentieth-century view of Rackham & Co. Ltd showing the North Western Arcade entrance. John Rackham appears in a street directory from 1882 trading as Rackham & Matthews at Bull Street. After William Matthews left, the business was bought by a Charles Richards who was then trading at Snow Hill. John Rackham left in 1898 but his name lived on, as the business (now styled as 'Linen, silk and woollen mercers') then extended into the nearby arcade. Richards also took over the Beehive in Albert Street and the Rackhams store was rebuilt and extended during the First World War.

During the Second World War, the Rackhams store suffered three bomb hits. In 1955 the store was bought by London retailer Harrods and two years later a massive seven-year, eight-phase, multi-million pound redevelopment began, the basis of which is still there today. The eight storeys, included twenty-six letable shops in the North Western Arcade and Windsor Arcade and an office block (Windsor House), made it one of the largest department stores in Britain. The famous ground floor food hall opened in 1966. This view, from the early 1970s, shows the Temple Row side, shortly after pedestrianisation. Margaret Tregoring's flower shop, next door, has since been demolished.

Above: A general view of the
Men's Clothing Department
at Rackhams, as featured
in the *Birmingham Sketch*
in April 1963. (Photo by
Willoughby Gullachsen.)

Left: An advertisement
for 'The Man's Shop' at
Rackhams, in the *Birmingham
Sketch*, April 1963.

Old Square, 10 February 1932 at 11.10 a.m., showing the construction of the new extension to Lewis's. By now it was a public company and had bought the neighbouring store of Newbury's. Lewis's was allegedly the first store in Britain to use electric light in a shop and to repair shoes and boots by machinery.

Lewis's in Bull Street, prior to pedestrianisation, 16 November 1971. They were responsible for introducing Father Christmas and his grotto to millions of children. By this time, the firm was owned by the fashion giant Sears and a management buyout took place in 1988.

A busy scene outside Lewis's, Corporation Street and Bull Street, 19 July 1955. However, as time went on, the store's fortunes declined. Reasons given at the time were its isolated position, competition from out-of-town shopping centres, high rates and lack of car parking. The Birmingham store closed in 1991.

Above: The junction of Bull Street and Colmore Row, with Steelhouse Lane to the left, around 1945. J.H. Dean's tailor's is prominent on the left; Freeman Hardy & Willis's footwear, opposite, with Burton's next door with a prominent advertising hoarding for their seventy-five shilling suit. A Boots chemists store, right, still has its windows boarded up from the war.

Below: Edward Greey (the second 'e' was dropped because he thought it would be a better trading name) was a former buyer at Lewis's who set up a fancy goods shop at No. 66 Bull Street in 1891. After his death in 1925, his sons built the well-known landmark store, seen here, which opened in 1926. In 1958 the family-run firm of Grey's sold out to Debenhams of London who also bought Marshall & Snelgrove in New Street and Stanley's in Colmore Row. Grey's was renamed Debenhams in 1973 and the building was given an £80,000 face lift. By 1974 it employed around 1,000 people though its staff turnover of 45 per cent was high. By the recession of the early 1980s, falling profits, high bus fares and the lack of development around the Snow Hill area, were reasons cited by Debenhams for the store's closure in 1983. It briefly reopened under the Edward Grey name, selling cut-price goods in Christmas 1984, then another Debenhams subsidiary, Hamley's toy shop, was based there in 1985 when it was the world's second largest toy shop until it faced serious competition from America's Toys R Us superstore which opened in Dale End in 1986. Debenhams, now part of the Burton group, was to make a comeback with a flagship superstore in Birmingham's new Bull Ring in 2003.

Above: The grand premises of Holliday & Son & Co., Warwick House, Nos 25–30 New Street. Later rebuilt in distinctive art deco-style in 1938 though not completed until 1956 due to the War, when it was occupied by the drapers Marshall & Snelgrove until closure in 1970. The shop is now occupied by a mobile phone company, though the remainder of the building was converted into a hotel.

Below: Founded by Charles Richards in 1870 and later taken over by his nephew and three grandsons, the Beehive in Albert Street originally sold 'stays, bonnets and ribbons by the yard' before it moved into carpets, furniture, bedding, hardware, china etc. Despite a bad fire in 1911, the store, known as a bit of a rabbit warren, thrived and was one of the first city stores to offer home deliveries with a motor vehicle in 1914. It was also well known for its Lamson cash tubes. Further extensions were made between the wars, but by 1967 the old building was in need of modernisation, so a modern larger Beehive opened in Priory Ringway on the corner of Corporation Street. By then it was the only surviving family-owned department store in the city centre. However, this new location proved not ideal for trade and, in 1971, the receivers were called in and after over a century of trading, the Beehive closed in 1972. Tesco took over the building the following year, selling non-food items.

Above: An early example of a majestic department store, pictured in 1913, when Crockford Grove & Sons had moved to these new premises at Nos 101-103 Bull Street. Note the entrance to Union Passage, right. One of the window posters boasts: 'the smartest collection of dainty blouses in the Midlands.' The firm ceased trading in 1923.

Opposite above: Robert Lee and George Longland founded the famous Broad Street store in 1903, to sell quality furniture and furnishings to upmarket Edgbaston households. The original site was a single shop, sited opposite the Hall of Memory at the junction where Paradise Circus now is. It included a basement workshop producing their own furniture. By 1909 they had bought their neighbouring businesses.

Opposite below: Lee Longlands moved to its current site, a floodlit art deco building in 1936, further up Broad Street at No. 224. It has been extended over the years and has the advantage of its own car park. Its unique location between the city centre and Five Ways suggests it has fared better than some of its rivals over the years.

LEE LONGLAND & C⁰ LTD.
COMPLETE HOUSE FURNISHERS

o o o

304 BROAD STREET
(OPPOSITE THE HALL OF MEMORY)
BIRMINGHAM
TELEPHONE :- MIDLAND 626- 627

(2 LINES)

WE ENCLOSE RECEIPT WITH THANKS AND SOLICIT YOUR FURTHER
VALUED ORDERS AND RECOMMENDATIONS

Above: Stanford & Mann's stationery store at No. 184 Broad Street where they operated from 1962-69. Their first store at No. 73 New Street (by the old Christ Church) was opened by Alfred Stanford and Edward Mann in 1888. After that area was rebuilt in the early 1900s, they returned to Galloway's corner where they were to remain until 1970, when again the area was knocked down. They later moved to Paradise Street opposite the Town Hall and then to New Street in 1990, before closing a few years later. In their heyday, they had branches in Harborne, Kings Heath, Erdington, Broad Street, Edmund Street and Suffolk Street as well as their own printing works.

Left: It's some time since these basket carriages were the standard means of local deliveries for shops like Stanford and Mann in the city centre. This carriage was thought to be the last one used in the city, up to the late seventies. In this photo from 1970 Tom Growcott was the delivery man.

The despatch department and local delivery of Barrow's Store, Corporation Street in 1924. A century earlier, it was founded by John Cadbury at No. 93 Bull Street, selling teas, spices, coffee and cocoa. J.C., as he was known, was an enterprising businessman who later went on to form Cadbury's chocolate factory at Bournville. He introduced the first large, plate glass windows to his shops where the teas and coffees could be better displayed and also employed a Chinaman, resplendent in national costume in order to attract custom.

Left: Barrow's Stores Restaurant advertisement, 1905. In 1849, John Cadbury's nephew, Richard Cadbury Barrow, took over the business and added sugar and general groceries to the range. Additional premises were built when Corporation Street was constructed in 1880, called Lancaster Buildings. Rapid expansion followed in the new century as can be seen from the advertisement for their new café in 1905.

Below: The original Barrow & Co. store at No. 93 Bull Street in 1865.

Above: The grocery department of the new Barrow's store at No. 95 Bull Street in 1924. At this time, they had cafés, kitchens, a bakery, confectionery and cooked meats departments. In 1931, the basement opened for the sale of crafts, china and glass.

Right: The bakery of Barrow's Store, 1924. Both the confectionery and cooked meat departments were supplied from here.

Above: Barrow's were renowned for their Christmas 'Goodwill Hampers'. There was a choice of eight different hampers ranging from a luxury hamper costing £7 7s to a children's hamper containing mainly sweets which cost £1 11s 6d.

Left: A view of the old Barrow's store in Corporation Street, opposite Rackhams in 1966. A modern Barrow's stores had been built in 1964 on the corner of Corporation Street and Bull Street. The Barrow family sold out to the Fitch Lovell 'Keymarkets' group in 1965, but by the early 1970s city centre grocery stores were considered to be out-dated and the store closed at Christmas 1973. Their building was later taken over by the national chain of Courts furniture.

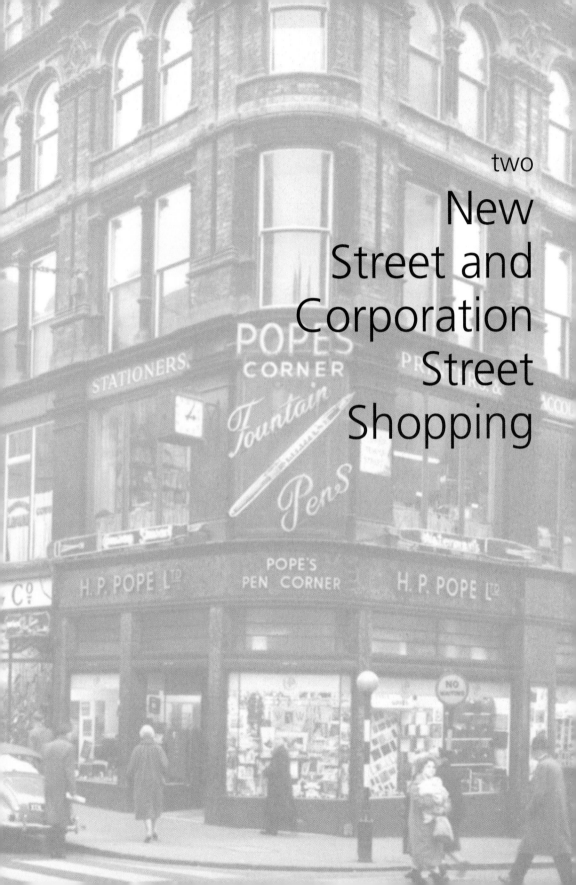

two

New Street and Corporation Street Shopping

Above: Pattisons corner. The café was a favourite meeting place for Birmingham shoppers, staying open to 9 p.m.

Right: Another favourite meeting place, under Nathan's clock.

Opposite above: An early view of one of the city's premier shopping streets, Corporation Street, with the Abyssinian Gold and Jewellery Co. prominent. The construction of Corporation Street in the late Victorian period, which involved the demolition of much unsavoury housing, is regarded as one of the main factors which led to the economic growth of the city centre.

Opposite below: A 1920s view of Corporation Street Burtons, (on the left of the photograph opposite Saxone Shoes). Parking on Corporation Street was a problem even then, judging by the notice with its unambiguous message 'No parking in this street'.

Midland Educational at Nos 41-43 Corporation Street, just down from Cherry Street. As well as its city centre store, Midland Ed. had shops in King Street, Sparkbrook and High Street Erdington.

James Wilson, booksellers, Hutton House, No. 151 Corporation Street, originally established in 1870.

Outside Dolcis Shoes on 18 August 1936 on the Bull Street/Corporation Street corner. Apparently the pedestrians are being 'educated about the special lights' which had just been introduced.

Corporation Street in June 1984 bedecked for the Rotary Convention at the NEC.

Above: A postcard view of New Street looking past Galloways corner to the shops on New Street.

Right: Hollingsworth, the tobacconists, at No. 122 New Street between Burlington Passage and Stephenson Street.

Opposite above: When winters were winters and Christmas shoppers needed plenty of warm clothing, Corporation Street two weeks before Christmas, 1981.

Opposite below: Aerial view of Corporation Street.

New Street, Birmingham

5 COMBRIDGE 5

BOOKSELLER LATE DENHAM STATIONER

LOWEST PRICES
FOR CASH
10 PER CENT OFF
FANCY GOODS

PRESENTS & PRIZES

LOWEST PRICES
FOR CASH
3d IN THE SHILLING
OFF BOOKS

COMBRIDGE   COMBRIDGE

Above: Some of New Street's best-remembered shops; Pope's Corner on the corner of Lower Temple Street, with Pope's stationers and pen shop, Day's shoe shop and Hudson's bookshop, on 5 January 1960.

Below: A close up of Pope's in the early 1900s.

Opposite: Views of the booksellers Combridges at Nos 4–5 New Street.

Above and below: Day's shoe shop around 1950, part of an evocative group of photos of the shop held in the Local Studies section of Birmingham Central Library.

Above: Manfield Shoes on the corner with Needless Alley in March 1972.

Below: Christmas shopping in New Street, 1984.

A.R. Thomas's shop in New Street taken from a copy of *Birmingham Faces and Places*. According to the accompanying article, 'Mr. Thomas's old curiosity shop in New Street may claim to be one of the best known in Birmingham and its proprietor is certainly one of the well-known faces in the city'.

Mr Thomas, the very image of the Victorian shopkeeper.

A night-time view of New Street close to the Corporation Street corner showing the offices of the *Birmingham Post*, and H. Greaves.

Dale, Forty and Co. 'appointed dealers for Bush Televisions' at No. 84 New Street, 11 March 1958. Other shops close by were the tobacconists at No. 81 and Connolly and Olivieri, the wine merchants.

Rex Johnson, jewellers. (Courtesy of Anthony Spettigue)

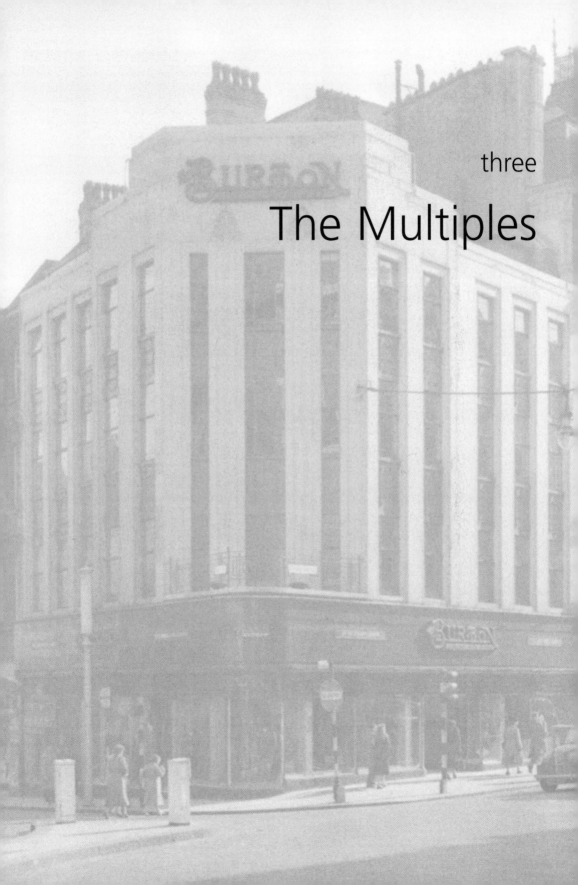

three

The Multiples

Above: On 21 January 1949 an empty Midland Red bus shelter awaits passengers in front of Littlewoods Mail Order stores at No. 135 New Street which was built on the site of the King Edward High School in 1936-7. Littlewoods later moved to new premises in High Street, designed by their own company and built in 1959-64.

Left: The Times Furnishing Co.'s distinctive eight-storey tower building, Nos 24 and 26 High Street, dates from 1936-38. It is now occupied by Waterstone's books. Seen here in the 1950s with the now demolished Burton's tailors building next door.

C & A Modes store at Nos 14, 16, 18, 20 Corporation Street in 1962 when an 'Economy Week' promotion was displayed in the windows. Founded in 1841 by Dutch brothers Clemens and August Brenninkmeyer, C & A Modes store opened on this site in 1926 offering mainly women's and children's outer garments at reasonable prices. In 1941 the store was destroyed by enemy action, so for a while they moved to New Street and High Street. Their new store opened in 1949 and was further extended in 1958 and 1969.

While C & A's Corporation Street store was being rebuilt in 1969, they traded at the former Henry's store in the Big Top, High Street until the store reopened in 1971. However the C & A group struggled in the highly competitive 1990s with more trendy fashion names such as Gap, Next, New Look and Hennes coming to prominence. The store closed in January 2001 as C & A disappeared from the British high street. Their store was then occupied by the James Beattie group until 2005.

The small Marks & Spencer shop, centre, with the 'for sale' sign in High Street. This shop had long counters on either side which were filled with haberdashery, chocolates, biscuits, toys, hardware, stationery and crockery, all for around a halfpenny or penny. Marks & Spencer were to acquire all the buildings to the left of their shop, including the Holborn Inn. Marks & Spencer's first Birmingham shop opened in 1898 on Snow Hill and by 1904 they were also at the Market Hall. To the right is a typical George Mason's grocers and a Warner's footwear shop.

The same scene, around 1960. The Marks & Spencer High Street shop was destroyed by enemy action in 1941 and for a while they traded at the former YMCA huts. After the war, the store was rebuilt and has since been extended several times since. It has benefited from corridor links with the Pavilions Shopping Centre which opened October 1987 on the site of the Co-operative. By 1993 it was the fifth largest Marks & Spencer in the world. A suburban food store was opened in Harborne in October 2000 and another food store in Colmore Row in 2003. They also have outlets at the Fort Retail Park and New Street Station.

Right: W.H. Smith & Son's bookshop at Nos 19-21 Corporation Street in 1923 featured stone reliefs of Walter Scott and William Shakespeare. The architect was George E. Pepper, renowned for his factory works such as Lucas's and Cannings. They moved to their larger, modern Union Street store in 1974.

Below: The Leeds-based firm of Montague Burton menswear was formed in 1900. The dual-entrance store seen here was on Corporation Street and Bull Street, in the 1950s. Shops on the west side of Bull Street included Finlay's tobacconist's; Shamrock Linen Co., drapers; J & F. Stone's lighting and Radio; Ryder's house, furnishers; J.T. Modes, costumiers; Barrow's stores; True-Form shoes and Hardy's house, furnishers. Today, Burton is part of the massive Arcadia group which includes TopShop, TopMan, Evans, Wallis, Miss Selfridge and Dorothy Perkins.

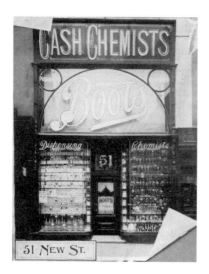

Boots Cash Chemists was at Nos 51–53 New Street on the corner of Bennett's Hill, 1920s. Jesse Boot from Nottingham founded the first store in 1849, selling herbal remedies. In 2006 the company merged with Alliance Unichem.

Another Boots Chemists' store, on the corner of Bull Street and Nos 2–8 Colmore Row (next to the Great Western Arcade), 1950s Note that the flag is flying over Grey's department store. Boots Chemists were also to be found in most of Birmingham's suburbs.

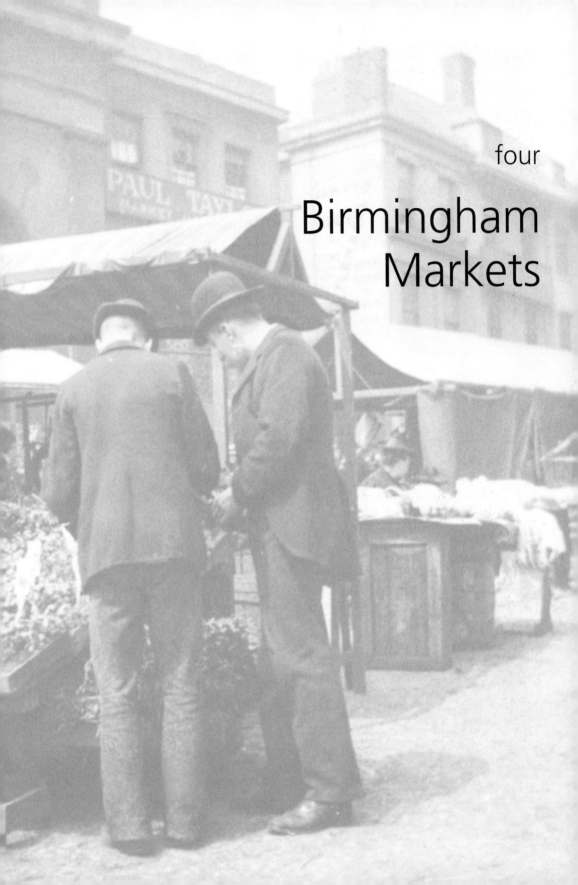

four

Birmingham Markets

Above: The Bull Ring flower market photographed by Percy Deakin on 7 May 1898. The flower market was held on Tuesdays, Thursdays and Saturdays. Right from the origins of Birmingham and the granting of the first market charter to Peter de Bermingham in 1166, the site of the markets have been the heart and centre of the town.

Left: The splendid Central Fountain in the Market Hall. It was placed in the centre of the Hall in 1851, sixteen years after the opening of the Market Hall itself but came to be regarded as a hindrance to trade and was later moved to Highgate Park.

A copy of a print in the Museum and Art Gallery showing the Market Hall and the corner of High Street and Bell Street in 1840.

The Market Hall decorated for the coronation of George VI, 1937. Three years later in September 1940 the Market Hall was to suffer a direct hit from a German incendiary bomb, destroying its famous and much-loved clock and much of the building's structure.

A Public Works Department photo of the Bull Ring Indoor Market on 20 August 1964. The ultra-modern lines of the then newly-built market appealed to sixties' Birmingham shoppers before eventually coming to look tired and outdated at the end of the nineties.

The retail market in 1964.

Outside the wholesale markets in Moat Row showing Italian women buying onions on 1 June 1901. Jamaica Row is in the background.

The Antiques Fair in the Rag market is still one of the best opportunities in the city to find something different.

Above: Kings Hall market, Old Square, in its closing days, photographed on 30 May 1961. The popular Mecca dance hall with its twice daily dancing was close by.

Left: The Kings Hall market, now deserted and on fire in 1962.

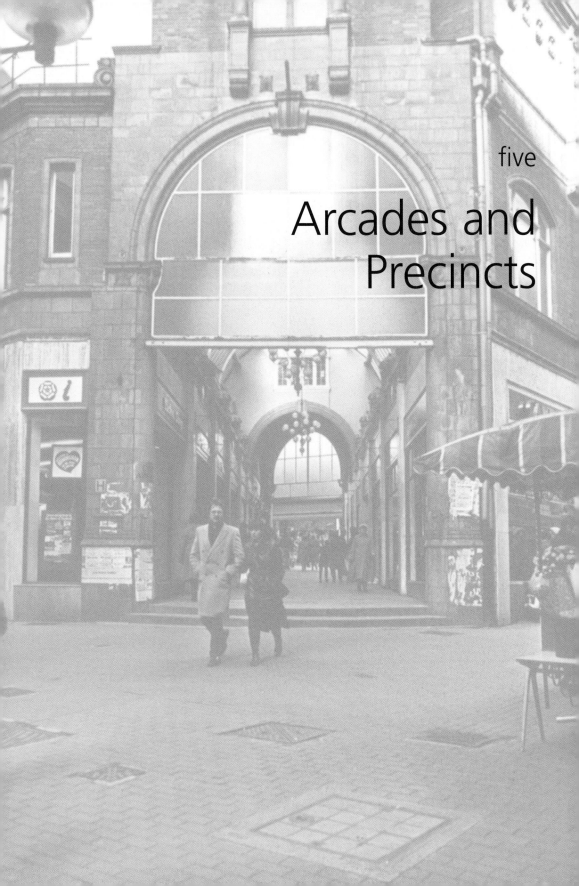

five

Arcades and Precincts

Shops under the impressively vaulted roof of Midland Arcade in the Edwardian period. The Midland Arcade was the last of the original covered city arcades to be built and the first to be lost when, as a result of a German bombing raid in April 1941, it was destroyed. Shoppers could enter the Arcade from New street and follow it through to the city arcades.

The Windsor Arcade with Evans and Matthews (furnishing, ironmongery and cutter), facing Rackhams, with Etam to the left of the entrance.

The New Street entrance to the Piccadilly Arcade on 27 May 1954. The van outside Samuels, the jewellers, and the Theatre Royal belongs to Sartorial Shops Ltd. The arcade was created out of the auditorium of the Picture House cinema after the cinema closed in 1926 and right up to today has housed a variety of small and independent shops. When this photo was taken, besides Samuels, the arcade appealed to the female shopper housing a milliners, a ladies' outfitters, a ladies' hairdressers, a florists, a wool shop and a needlework shop.

The clean lines of the New Street shopping arcade in the sixties showing how the city's architects and planners looked at the shopping experience.

Above: The opposite side of the City Arcade featuring Cantors furniture, carpets and electrical goods shop.

Right: The entrance to the City Arcade on 18 January 1984. The Birmingham information and tourist shop on the left of the entrance was there for many years.

Opposite above: North-Western Arcade looking down to Corporation Street with Rackhams' windows on the right-hand side. On the left-hand side women shoppers peruse the chocolates in the windows of Thornton's and visualise their men in the shirts and suits in the display in the windows of Malcolm Brooks, men's outfitters.

Opposite below: City Arcade, Union Street, on 3 October 1974 showing the Birmingham Dairies coffee shop and the hatters, Bricknells.

The splendid Great Western Arcade, June 1982. Probably the city's finest shopping arcade and passageway, the purpose-built arcade was opened on 19 August 1876. It was constructed over the tunnel leading into Snow Hill station and originally housed thirty-eight shops on the ground level and fifty-six offices on the gallery level.

Great Western Arcade, January 1988. The arcade was extensively and sensitively refurbished in the eighties and it became the home of many of the city's more upmarket shops.

The Colmore Row entrance to the Great Western Arcade, January 1984, showing Barnby's toy shop and the Kardomah coffee shop. A notice explains that Hardwicks are about to move.

Mansells clothes shop and Something Different, in the Great Western Arcade, April 1988. Latterly the arcade has struggled to keep its upmarket reputation and shops in the face of the new Bull Ring and the Mailbox developments.

The clean lines of the New Street shopping centre, the Pallasades, 12 July 1979.

Martineau Square, 1975, at the time a popular resting place for shoppers and office workers.

Underground kiosks in the subway between Hurst Street and Hill Street, March 1961. More than most cities, Birmingham embraced the concept of the separation of the car and pedestrians in post-war redevelopment sending pedestrians and shoppers underground. The city's underpasses and below-road level squares housed a number of shopping outlets all now swept away with the closing of most of the city centre underpasses.

A suburban precinct, The Circle, Kingstanding, on 15 November 1967, typical of many pedestrian-friendly local shopping areas.

Above: Entrance to the City
Plaza on Corporation Street on
2 February 1995. The City Plaza
along with the Arcadian Centre, the
Pallasades and the Pavilions were
at the forefront of the Birmingham
shopping centre revolution of
the nineties only in turn to be
overtaken by the Mailbox and the
new Bull Ring.

Left: One of the city's longest
established businesses (1843), John
Hollingsworth & Sons, tobacconists,
photographed by Anthony
Spettigue in April 2007.

six

Gone but not Forgotten

Above: Birmingham's Big Top office site under construction in High Street and corner of New Street in 1955. Note the double-fronted Co-operative Store in High Street and The Times Furnishing building.

Opposite above: Harrison's 'Corner' Optician's on the east side of Snow Hill, with J.H. Dean's tailors, established in 1860. This block was looking rather run down when photographed in 1957. Note the Wesleyan & General Assurance's old building and the Gaumont cinema on Steelhouse Lane.

Opposite below: Opposite the side of Snow Hill railway station in the early 1950s was an interesting range of shops including Snow Hill post office; NEP electrical appliances; a billiards room; a telephone company; Blue Star restaurant; Jennings' optician's; Timpson's shoes and Burnard's tools.

A busy scene in High Street, Bull Ring on the right of St Martin's parish church, 29 July 1952. From right to left are Hawkesford tobacconist's; Wheatlands and Leeks house furnisher's; Arthur Raymond, butcher, then the massive Woolworth's store, (later to move to New Street on the site of the old Theatre Royal by Piccadilly Arcade).

Roadworks in High Street, 29 July 1952, with Oswald Bailey's Army & Navy stores dominating the corner with Moor Street.

Shops on the corner of the east side of Moor Street and Bull Ring, prior to demolition, 7 August 1955. To the right of Moor Street station, above the young-looking policeman, is the white-stoned finish of the Woolpack Hotel. A couple of doors further along, with the tall chimney, is the Tamworth Arms public house. Cresswell's shoe shop is on the corner next door to a variety of shops within Nelson House. Next door is Campbell's house furnisher proclaiming a 'demolition sale' and Hobbies tool shop at No. 14 and a Shelfield's advertising hoarding placed over the former James Glover agricultural engineers premises.

Steelhouse Lane at the intersection of Snow Hill and Bull Street, early 1950s. A Savings Week promotion was due to take place with a target of £12 million. This view shows Grey's other department store at Nos 5-6, just round the corner from their main Bull Street store.

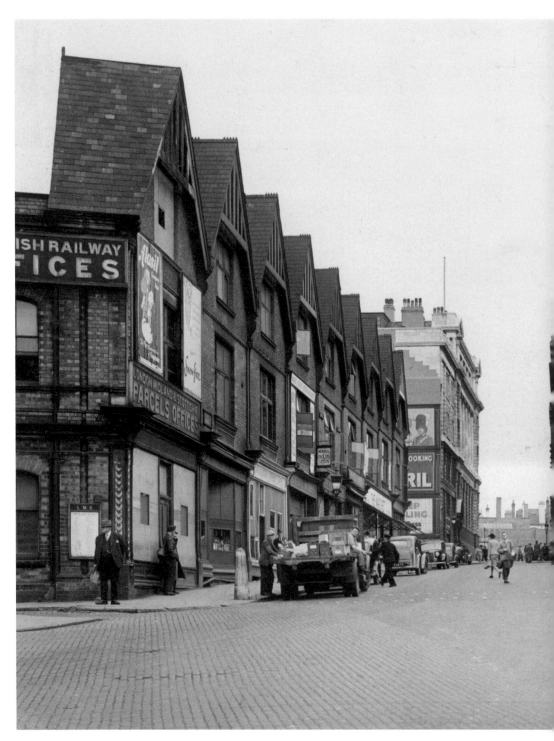

Looking up Worcester Street towards New Street in 1946, the remains of the bombed Market Hall dominate. On the left, many shops' windows are still boarded up despite the War ending the previous year. A varied row of shops including the LMS parcels office, with a passage next door leading to

New Street Station; Fred King's fishing tackle; Worcester Street café; Robert & Morris seed merchant's; Henry Woolf, watchmaker; Walter Glover, fruiterer; then the Magnet, clothes shop. Next to the building with the small dome is Loo Bloom tailors' which stood on the junction of Phillips Street.

At the top of the east side of Snow Hill towards Bull Street stood the NB Shoe Warehouse advertising a sale at 'Slaughter prices' with 25 to 75 per cent reductions.

A view from 1887 of Thomas Smith & Co.'s Stationery shop at No. 6 Cherry Street, on the corner of Cannon Street.

Opposite above: No mistaking the sign for Williams the Hatter at No. 54 Smallbrook Street in 1884. This view was taken from the Horsefair looking towards Hurst Street and shows the Bull's Head hotel, right.

Below: A 1946 view of Smallbrook Street looking towards Hurst Street showing Isaac Thomas (later Lea Morris) house furnishers shop on the corner of Wrottesley Street. Shops opposite included Morton's shoe shop; Malcolm, confectioners; Joseph Sanley's fishing tackle; SMC (Shirt Manufacturing Company); Johnson, jewellers then the Black Lion public house. The shored-up building by Smart's butchers on the corner of Hill Street acts as a reminder of the extent of the bomb damage suffered in this area which was one of the first to be redeveloped post-war.

A view from 1911 of Symington & Edwards, fancy draper's shop at No. 100 Bull Street, next to Union Passage.

The Windsor Arcade in Bull Street with Rackhams next door on the corner of Temple Row, early 1950s. Lower down on the corner of Corporation Street is Burton's tailors.

Shops in Bull Street between Corporation Street and Temple Row, early 1950s. Dolcis shoes, with a neon advertising roof sign for Ascot Geysers gas water heaters; Sawer's fishmongers; Evans & Matthews hardware and Rackhams on the corner, next to the Windsor Arcade.

Left: The quaintly-named 'Fifty Shilling Tailors' shop on Bull Street with Morton's shoe shop next door, early 1950s.

Below: Business looks a little slow at the January sale of 1963 in Lower Bull Street. Shops included McConville, gowns; Etam, hosiers; Kendall & Sons, umbrellas; Child, jewellers; Burton, tailors; Boots the Chemists; Simpson, fishmonger, established 1790 who had other shops in Moseley, Edgbaston and Bristol Street; Peter Conway, tailors; Singer Sewing Machines and Eve Brown, ladies clothing. Just out of view to complete the line up were Zissman Bros, outfitters; Thornton's confectionery and Preedy, newsagents at the junction with Dale End.

Above: In the 1960s when the car ruled supreme in the city centre, Birmingham's shoppers were driven off the streets into underpasses which later became dark, dingy and dangerous places – a trend that, thankfully, is now being reversed. This underpass outside Lewis's in Bull Street and Corporation Street already looks run down, *c.* 1968.

Right: Plenty of books on offer at James Wilson's bookshop (established 1870) at Hutton House, 151 Corporation Street. Identifiable books on sale are *Nuttall's Dictionary* for 1926 at 5s (25p). Books, coloured prints and autographs were purchased for cash. Wilson later moved to Broad Street near Five Ways.

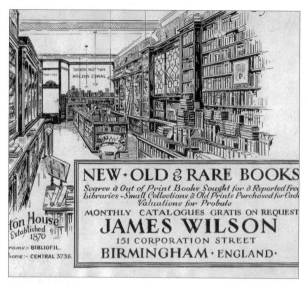

Above: Inside James Wilson's.

Below: The Snow Hill branch of Galloway's chemist's, *c.* 1929. Gordon Stewart Galloway opened his first shop in Colmore Row in 1921.

Opposite, top: Galloway's Chemists at No. 79 New Street and Victoria Square *c.*1931. This well-known shop gave its name to the whole block of shops in this area, built in 1901 to replace Christ Church, Galloway's Corner, until demolition in 1970.

Opposite, middle and bottom: Two interior views of Galloway's Chemists shop in New Street from 1931.

Above: Christmas cards on sale at Graves Gallery in December 1969. This view of Christ Church Passage was taken from Waterloo Street looking down towards New Street, not long before this block of shops, including Galloway's Corner, were demolished. Next door to Graves is the Copper Kettle restaurant, then Rowans clothes shop which stood on the corner of New Street.

Opposite above: E.F. Hudson's bookshop at No. 116 New Street was the city's major bookshop for many years prior to being taken over by Dillon's (later Waterstone's). This view dates from 1952 when Hudson's Technical and Scientific department was over at Burlington Passage. This store always had the feel of a rabbit warren to it. Many famous people visited here for book signings.

Below: Looking from Victoria Square down towards Stephenson Street, many signs advertise Connolly & Olivieri Ltd, Wine Merchants at Nos 50-51 Pinfold Street in May 1954. Next door is Ted Williams, tailors, then the Dale Forty piano shop by the HMV sign. Their main entrance was on New Street.

Easy Row as seen from Paradise Street in 1946. To the right of the Woodman Inn, with its wonderful wooden Woodman carving, is Thomas Armstrong, furnishers; Civic Radio Services (when you could rent a radio in the days when hardly anyone had a television); Watson & Glover, opticians; Bellamy & Wakefield, chemists.

A view of Rogers & Priestley's music
warehouse on Colmore Row between
Newhall Street and Colmore Row, *c.* 1920.

This view of shops by Galloway's Corner
in Victoria Square was taken from the
Town Hall around 1969, shortly before
demolition. From left to right we see
Harry Payne's shoe repairers; Abbey
National Building Society; Winchester
House which housed mainly insurance and
state agents; J. Lyon's tea and coffee shop,
probably the city's best known and most
popular meeting place for a generation of
Brummies; Ruth's Place, club; R.S. McColl,
confectioners and local landmark Galloway's
Chemist's on the corner of New Street.

The Kardomah Coffee House on Colmore Row in the shadow of Grey's on Bull Street. For many years the café was situated in New Street and when the Great Western Arcade was rebuilt, it opened here.

On the corner of Broad Street and Bishopsgate Street in April 1958, the Skefko Ball Bearing Co. adjoins Edgbaston House; Block & Anderson, office machines and next to the Immanuel parish church is Helen Parker, children's outfitters. To the left of the church can be seen some of Birmingham's well-known car showrooms, Hangers and P.J. Evans.

Supermarkets in the city centre are nothing new as this view shows the Fine Fare supermarket in the Bull Ring Shopping Centre Manzoni Gardens. They were at this site for three years from when the redeveloped Bull Ring opened in 1964.

George Heath car showrooms occupied two floors on the corner of Lower Temple Street and Stephenson Street, 1939. Models available included Austin, Rolls Royce, Humber, Hillman, Bentley, Commer and Rootes. They later moved to a more convenient location in Newhall Street.

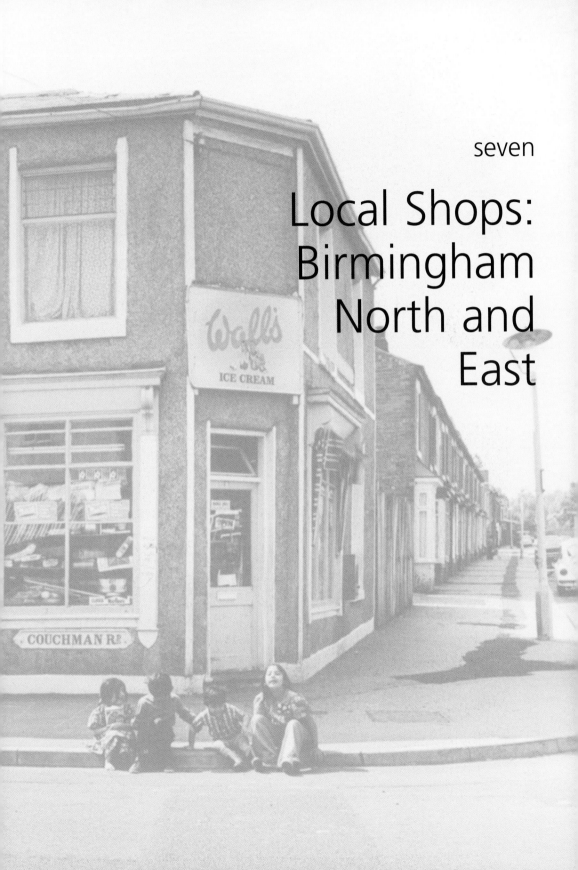

seven

Local Shops:
Birmingham
North and
East

Above: A favourite shopping centre for the residents of Hockley, Winson Green and Brookfields, Lodge Road, Hockley is universally known as 'The Flat'. This bustling group of shops was on its last legs in 1977 as redevelopment and road-building were to cut off the road from its erstwhile customers.

Left: H.V. Smith's the bakers, a real survivor both in terms of location, still in Lodge Road and as another dying breed, the independent baker. Smith's have just three branches left in the city. (Courtesy of Anthony Spettigue, 2007)

Above: Rees and Felix, selling bedding, carpets and household linen at their shop on the corner of Icknield Street and New Spring Street in 1930.

Right: Birmingham's Jewellery Quarter attracts not just local shoppers but also shoppers from around the West Midlands region and further afield, looking for bargains on rings and every other item of jewellery. This is the Diamond Centre in 1987. (Courtesy of Anthony Spettigue)

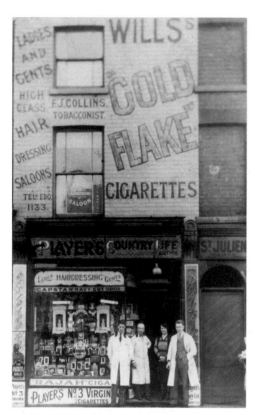

Left: The tobacconist, Fred Collins at No. 379 Dudley Road next to the Yorkshire Grey pub. The Dudley Road has, despite many, many upheavals over the years, managed to retain a lot of its vibrancy as a shopping destination, latterly largely through the entrepreneurial efforts of its ethnic shopkeepers.

Below: West Birmingham Garage and group of shops on the Dudley Road.

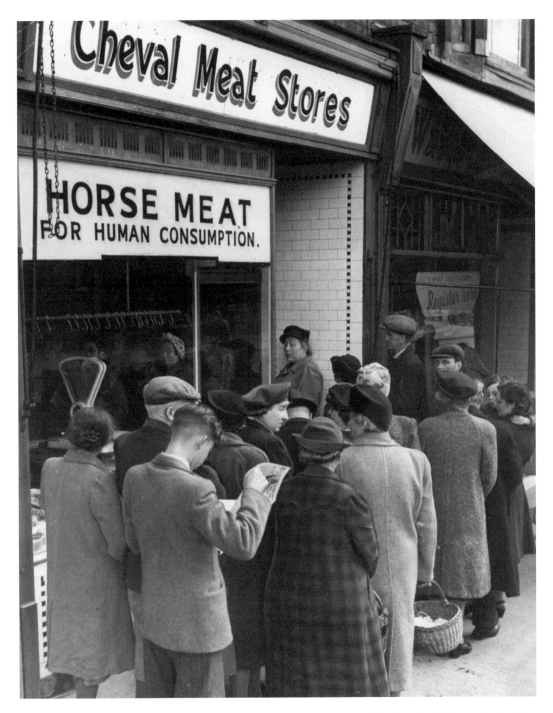

The wording on the back of the photograph attributes the location of this butcher's shop to the Dudley Road but it has proved difficult to find exactly where it was and when the photo was taken. The Central Library would be very pleased to be helped with any information.

Harry Smith's traditional ironmongers, one of a dying breed in the face of supermarket competition. Originally established in 1824 the business occupies the corner of Key Hill. (Courtesy of Andrew Spettigue)

Soho Road shops in 1985. The profusion of fruit and vegetables displayed outside West Indian and Asian shops is now a common sight right through the city's suburbs.

A postcard view of the Birchfield Road. The shop on the right is Newells, agents for BSA bicycles 'perfect in every part'.

Perry Barr shopping centre, January 1967.

Cambridge House antiques at No. 168 Gravelly Lane, Erdington on the corner with Somerset Road and just along from Tower Carpets which was previously Tower Cycles. (Courtesy of Andrew Spettigue)

The Parade, Sutton Coldfield, perhaps not so dominant a shopping destination for shoppers on the north of the city as it was when this photo was taken, but still always pretty busy.

Part of Erdington High Street shortly before the Coronation on 28 May 1953. New Street is to the right and the shops include Williams and Sons, spirit merchants. Despite the best efforts of local traders and the City Council Erdington High Street has lost its traditional and specifically local feel.

Just down from the High Street and past Erdington library a M. & Butler off license – an 'offie' – in Orphanage Road, Erdington, in July 1961.

Central Square, Erdington, 22 August 1966.

The Circle, Kingstanding Road   PN3567

A postcard view of the shops at the Circle, Kingstanding.

Barnes the bakers on Potters Hill, Aston, *c.*1920, photographed by Alfred Juggins, Lozells Road.

Aston Wallpaper House on the Birchfield Road.

Aston Station Stores at Nos 307-311, Lichfield Road just across the road from the station. The building on the right is the Swan Pool Tavern. The Aston Station Stores was selling carpets, rugs and lino and offered a service re-tyreing pram wheels, (not a service provided today)! Next door was a tobacconist's.

Opposite above: Shop on Whitehead Road, Aston, advertising 'Red Diamond Cash Stamps here'.

Opposite below: Newtown Row/Aston High Street on 22 May 1967 looking towards the Bartons Arms and the Aston Hippodrome and showing the widening of the A34, which was to wipe out all the remaining traditional shops on both sides of the road.

A branch of Freeman, Hardy and Willis at No. 1125 Warwick Road, Acocks Green.

Shops on Station Road, Acocks Green, on 8 February 1956.

Not the most sensitive of shop fronts, this photograph depicts a group of shops on the Shirley Road at Acocks Green on 13 October 1976. To the left there is an estate agent which combined with charity shops and 'pound shops' have changed the feel of suburban shopping centres and high streets.

The Swan Indoor Market, Yardley, September 1984.

High Point Corner and Thimble Mill Lane, 30 January 1964.

James's general stores at No. 70 Parkfield Road, Alum Rock. Note the adverts for Green Shield stamps and for 'hot bread now on Sundays.'

The Nechells Park Road branch of the Co-op next to the Soldiers Return pub, June 1975.

The Willis grocery and provisions store in, not surprisingly, Willis Street, Nechells. The shop window features adverts for such long-forgotten brands as Epps Cocoa, Milkmaid milk, Vinolia soap, and Farrow A1 mustard. Golden days!

A group of shops on the Nechells Park Road on 22 March 1971. One of the shops, Bullivants, the drapers, was in business right up to this summer (2007) but sadly after over a hundred years of trading has closed down and the shop is scheduled to become a dental practice.

In the days when you could safely leave your bike unlocked when you went into a shop, here two cyclists have left their bikes to look at what was new in the cycling world in McGauleys cycle shop at No. 220 Great Lister Street. The cycle shop had previously belonged to T.H. James, whose name still appears above the shop. Further down the road the photo shows a butcher's, formerly the Great Lister Street Meat market and a branch of Timpsons.

Another group of shops in Great Lister Street this time on the corner of Cromwell Street in March 1960. Shops include: the chemists Bannister and Thatcher, Taylors the butcher's, Mrs Dora Haynes grocery shop and Mrs Aston, pastry cook.

Four young Asian friends pose for the camera in the road outside the general stores on the corner of Couchman Road and Clodeshall Road, Saltley, in July 1980.

Opposite above: Shops in Revesby Walk, the new modern future of shopping, taken away from the high street and traffic-free.

Opposite below: Saltley Market Hall on the Washwood Heath Road coming up to Christmas 1987, typical of a dying breed of suburban market halls across the city.

Right: Gem Street, Aston Street end around 1912–1913.

Below: Aston Street, Gosta Green, on 11 February 1932. It is just possible to make out that the shop partly hidden by the horse and cart and advertising Hovis was Cadwallader's bakery. This was situated at No. 98 Aston Street which was next to the passageway called Reeds Opening. Aston Street at one time boasted virtually every kind of shop you could want and all on the doorstep for shoppers living nearby.

Aston Street ran from Vauxhall Street to Gosta Green, shops include Woolfs and W.J. Baron on the corner of Sheep Street.

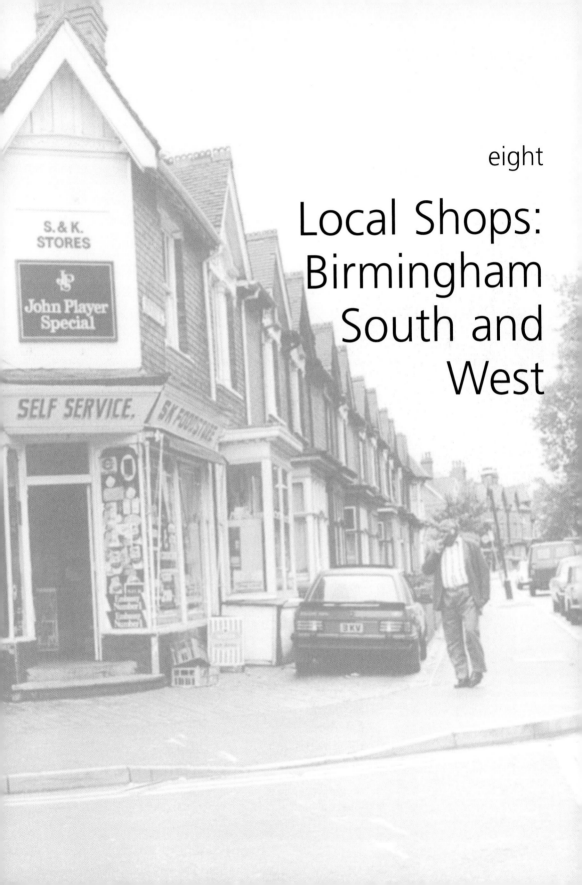

eight

Local Shops: Birmingham South and West

C. Green and Sons at No. 10, the Bull Ring, selling dog requisites, fancy leather goods and 'seasons goods'. The photo dates from about 1930. Other premises in the now-vanished small street were the pub, The Old Red Lion, a baker's, a fish and chip shop, a branch of Avery's repairing scales, a hop merchant's and a tailor's. All you need in life really.

Digbeth always had its share of interesting shops. Here in the thirties, next to the Old Crown pub was Rodways restaurant and cake shop next to F. Bickerstaff, milliners, at No. 185a Deritend.

Above and below: Jacksons, tobacconists, at No. 67 Digbeth High Street between Rea Street and Mill Lane.

Shops on the north side of Islington Row in 1958, including the house furnishers, Whitakers; the decorators, Brecknells; Neales the butcher's, the PDSA and a newsagent, Broadleys. This block of shops was soon to be demolished to make way for the Edgbaston shopping centre which in the way of retail development in the city is soon to be redeveloped itself.

The new-look Edgbaston shopping centre in the early 1970s with Hagley Road on the left. In 2007, it is to be demolished and rebuilt.

Monument Road shops in 1958 from the Nags Head public house. In this block were H.E. Haynes, butcher; A.E. Ayers and Sons, bakers; Atkin, newsagents; a toyshop, F.G. Robinson; Cyril Halbeard, a cooked meat dealer; The Jewel Box; D. Rogers, shopkeeper, and a hairdressers F. Fowler with the now familiar rotating sign outside.

The perhaps fancifully-named Sunfruit Stores on the corner of Sun Street West and Summer Road on 24 November 1960. Notice the advert for Corona pop. All the area was to be redeveloped as part of the Lea Bank scheme.

A reminder of a long-forgotten era – a china shop, Tulletts, pictured in Edwardian days. The shop moved around between two premises on the Moseley Road at Highgate, also at No. 70 High street Aston and No. 170 Alcester Road by Moseley village.

Shops on the west side of Gooch Street, Highgate cum Balsall Heath, in 1966 shortly before demolition. The group features a coffee shop, the Gooch Street Exchange and a turf accountants, (the posh name for a bookies), Bob Cutlers.

An earlier view of premises in Gooch Street, this time from 1955. Next to the Triangle cinema on the corner of Conybere street, were a suburban branch of Woolworths, Jigs and Tools and Leonard Ellis, film accessories.

Tom Hughes 'the butcher at the top of the street' on the corner of Edward Road and Wenman Street in 1970. You could ring your orders through to the shop on CAL 0922.

Court Road, Balsall Heath, with H. Betts, gentleman's outfitters, and H. Jones, radio and electrical repairs, next door to the electricity supply station.

The Balsall Heath branch of the Co-op on 8 June 1959.

A branch of Wrensons the grocers, Ladypool Road and Alder Road, Balsall Heath, on 8 February 1952.

The changing nature of Birmingham's retail shops is shown in the rise of Asian-owned corner and local shops, working long hours in family-run businesses Asian traders have given a new-found vitality to the small local shop and provided a measure of competition for the supermarkets and chains. This particular local shop is on the corner of Edward and Harbury roads in Balsall Heath and is pictured in the 1980s.

Above: The aptly-named Coles Corner Cycles, on the corner of Bowyer Street and Coventry Road, Bordesley, 1958. The building on the opposite corner was William McGeoch and Co., electrical engineers who were displaying their vacancies outside.

Below: A motorcycle dealers, Beacon Accessories, on the corner of the Stratford Road and Kyotts Lake Road in Sparkbrook next door to Kim's Café and the long-established Mason Stores (1912). For many years until very recently the premises were used by Vale-Onslow motorcycles run by probably Birmingham's oldest proprietor.

TASCOS branch No. 18 Yardley Wood Road near the corner with Bondfield Road. The Ten Acres and Stirchley Co-operative Society was a major presence in the south of the city. Three other major outlets, Baines, Timothy Whites and George Masons make up the remainder of the block.

A rare glimpse of winter sun illuminates the recently-built Cregoe Street shopping centre, Lee Bank, in January 1974.

Above: A postcard view of one of Birmingham's best suburban shopping streets, High Street, Kings Heath.

Right: A specially commissioned view of one of the small shops which greatly add to the diversity of the shops in Kings Heath. This is Nutts sewing machine shop at No. 5 Poplar Road. The business has been established for twenty-two years, but the building goes back to the nineteenth century when it began life as a china shop. (Courtesy of Anthony Spettigue)

Above: Another really local shop in Poplar Road, Contrasts the florists, the family business of Neville and Jackie Summerfield. Contrasts was opened in 1985, previously being a greengrocer's shop. (Courtesy of Andrew Spettigue)

Left: Up until its closure several weeks before the publication of this book, Sage Wholefoods on the Alcester Road in Moseley was a Mecca for devotees of organically-grown food. The garden at the rear of the shop was a real gem. Birmingham is not over-endowed with organic shops. Apart from Sage which was established in the 1970s and The Friends of the Earth shop in Allison Street near the city centre, Bournville is the only other location with 'alternative food shops'. (Courtesy of Andrew Spettigue)

The Treasure Trove, a well-loved store on the Pershore Road in Cotteridge three days before Christmas 1953. As its clock said 'The right time… to look around'. It boasted half an acre of show space. Customers delighted in browsing around its curios before it went the way of many such stores in the eighties to be replaced by a tyre shop and a supermarket.

Left: A 2007 view of an old business, Louise of Bournville at No. 43 Sycamore Road selling toys, greeting cards and flowers. (Courtesy of Anthony Spettigue)

Below: Sam Carpenter's television shop on the Bristol Road in Selly Oak looking out of town as it looked on 12 March 1957.

Right: Rossiter's, Birmingham's first organic butcher's, on the Mary Vale Road in Bournville. (Courtesy of Anthony Spettigue, 1999)

Below: Definitely not one of the most salubrious of shop fronts! These shops in Egghill Lane, Nothfield, were photographed by the City's Engineers Department.

A family butcher and baker, 'Baker's Choice', on the Northfield Road, Harborne in 1986.

Crusty's bakery at No. 4 St Stephens Road, Selly Park, one of the oldest bakeries in the city, having operated in the city for over seventy years. (Courtesy of Andrew Spettigue)

Shops on the south side of The Green, Kings Norton on 11 June 1937. The photograph shows the
Kings Norton Electrical Co., radio and television engineers with Edward Andrews' ironmonger's
shop to the left of the Esperanto motor car.

A view taken from the Grosvenor shopping centre, Northfield, of a mixture of shopping
developments from the thirties (left) and the sixties (right) along Bristol Road South at the
junction with Church Road, 1981.

An early sixties' view of A.H. Bibb's newsagent and 'circulating library' on the Northfield Road corner with Tennal Road, Harborne.

An ironmongers, Andrews & Sons, and a seed merchant, Sandersons, on the Bristol Road South corner with Sylvan Avenue captured on film on 23 February 1954.

A mixed group of shops on Hagley Road west between White Road and Hollybush Grove in Quinton. The block includes Taylor's furniture shop advertising 'Fireside chairs for 83s 6d', Dallaways fishmongers, Stutelys chemists, a jewellers and Suzanne's florist's. The photo was taken on 12 November 1953.

Nos 93-107 Blandford Road, Quinton on 31 July 1959. From left to right on the photo are a branch of the Co-op, Helen's drapers, a grocer's, Walkers, Standley's ironmongers and Andrews' newsagents.

Another varied group of suburban shop, this time on Hagley Road West between College Road and Ridgacre Road, Quinton. There was a hairdressers, W.B. Law, a corn and seed merchants A.W. Slim, Lowe's, tobacconists and Anne's café advertising Barber tea.

Shops on Wood Lane, Bartley Green photographed on 28 September 1959. This new development featured from right to left Cole's Mitchell & Butler off license, J.W. Francis, grocer; G. Boyce, butcher; McLean's newsagent's, A.G. Horne, draper; and Grainger and Grainger, greengrocer.

Right: And finally two real echoes of Birmingham's old shops; Hall's glass, china and hardware shop was established in 1874 and had various premises along the Dudley Road including as well as the china shop, two milliners shops.

Below: The best known 'old' shops in the city, the back-to-back premises on the corner of Inge Street and Hurst Street recently restored by the National Trust. If you want to see what a traditional sweet shop or a tailor's looked like pay the Back-to-Backs a visit.

Other local titles published by Tempus

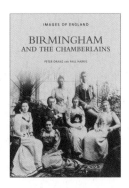

Birmingham and the Chamberlains
PETER DRAKE AND PAUL HARRIS

The Chamberlains – father Joe and sons Austen and Neville – are probably the country's best-known political family. Synonymous with Birmingham, they achieved both local fame and fortune. Together, they transformed late Victorian Birmingham into 'the best-governed city in the world'. This work provides a fascinating insight into the Chamberlain's legacy

978 07524 4492 5

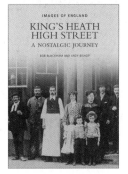

King's Heath High Street: A Nostalgic Journey
BOB BLACKHAM AND ANDY BISHOP

This fascinating selection of more than 200 archive photographs shows the ways in which King's Heath has developed over the centuries from its rural origins into the thriving suburb of today. Offering the most comprehensive photographic record of King's Heath High Street to date, this book will stir nostalgic memories in the minds of older King's Heath residents and provide younger residents with a unique glimpse of life in King's Heath as it used to be.

978 07524 4481 9

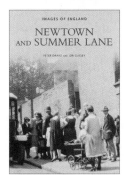

Newtown and Summer Lane
PETER DRAKE AND JON GLASBY

This book seeks to rectify a curious anomaly in the published records of Birmingham's history: references to Summer Lane and Newtown are rarely seen in published accounts of the city. The book also includes a pictorial account of a leading Birmingham voluntary organisation known as the Birmingham Settlement. It will be an important record for those who have lived and worked there and it will put on the historical map an area that has until now been largely neglected by the historians.

978 0 7524 4197 9

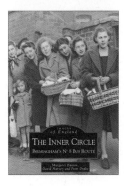

The Inner Circle: Birmingham's No. 8 Bus Route
PETER DRAKE, MARGARET HANSON AND DAVID HARVEY

This superb collection of over 200 old photographs illustrates the changes that have been seen along the Inner Circle bus route over the years. It also shows the buses that have worked on it so it is guaranteed to fascinate bus enthusiasts but will also have huge appeal for the thousands of Brummies who have travelled the route. This is an unusual book with wide appeal for anyone interested in Birmingham history.

978 0 7524 2636 5

If you are interested in purchasing other books published by Tempus, or in case you have difficulty finding any Tempus books in your local bookshop, you can also place orders directly through our website

www.tempus-publishing.com